Overlook Much
Correct a Little

"99 Words to Live By"

A series of fine gift books that presents inspirational words by renowned authors and captivating thinkers. Thought-provoking proverbs from many peoples and traditions complete each volume's collection.

"99 Words to Live By" explores topics that have moved and will continue to move people's hearts. Perfect for daily reflection as well as moments of relaxation.

Published in the United States by New City Press
202 Cardinal Rd., Hyde Park, NY 12538
©2007 New City Press (English translation)

Translated by Eugene Selzer
from the original German edition
Güte mit Klugheit gepaart
©2000 Verlag Neue Stadt, Munich.

Cover design by Leandro De Leon

Library of Congress Cataloging-in-Publication Data:
John XXIII, Pope, 1881-1963
[Güte--mit Klugheit gepaart. English]
Overlook much, correct a little: 99 sayings by John XXIII /
Hans-Peter Röthlin, editor; translated by Eugene Selzer.
    p. cm. -- (99 words to live by)
ISBN-13: 978-1-56548-261-6 (hardcover : alk. paper)
ISBN-13: 978-1-56548-255-5 (paper : alk. paper)
    1. Christian life--Catholic authors--Miscellanea. I. Röthlin,
Hans-Peter.
II Title.
BX2350.3.J5813   2007
242--dc22   2006030945

Printed in Canada

Overlook Much
Correct a Little

99 Sayings
by John XXIII

edited by
Hans-Peter Röthlin

New City Press
Hyde Park, New York

"Good Pope John" — shortly after his unexpected election in 1958, this is the name Catholics, Christians of other confessions and people outside the ecclesiastical world gave to John XXIII. As pope, Angelo Roncalli (1881–1963) made history with the Second Vatican Council and opened the Church to a new age of dialogue, yet he always remained a man of the people. He conquered hearts with his simple charm, his trust in God and his good humor.

Much of what he said still rings true today. In this collection, you will find words of wisdom that invite meditation even as they bring a frequent smile. These brief sayings convey disarmingly simple and kind yet indispensable advice. At the same time they reveal a profound union with God. Long before he became pope, John XXIII wrote from his daily experience.

His quiet musings, which expressed what contained meaning for him, can serve as a compass as you try to navigate our hectic, noisy culture. They invite you to look at things with greater calm and detachment.

You will find these 99 Sayings a comforting and encouraging foundation for your life now and in the future.

Hans-Peter Röthlin

Every beginning
fills the heart with hope.

Life makes
youthful dreams come true.
Every young person
should have a dream,
a dream destined
to become awesome reality.

What will become of me? Will I become a proficient theologian, a great jurist, a rural pastor or a poor, simple priest? But why do I trouble myself about all this? I must become none of these or more than these, however God will have it. God is everything to me. He will make sure that my striving for honor and my desire to look good before others comes to nothing.

On the eve of ordination

Everything I do
I will do as though
I were in the world
to accomplish that alone.

Ever to be occupied
but never to hurry,
that is heaven on earth.

Christian faith is this:
serenity and inner calm
while offering oneself to God.

I have never known
a pessimist to accomplish
anything useful for the world.

Do not
undertake too much.
A peaceful,
calm search for the good
is enough for each day,
each hour.
At all times
avoid immoderation
and impatience.

The believer
is never fearful.
He or she is
not a pessimist.
Faith is the serenity
that comes from God.

If God made darkness,
it was to intensify the light.

I will try
not to put off
urgent matters
yet still preserve
the calm necessary
for things to turn out well....
One who pushes too hard
gets nowhere.

Just for today...

Just for today I will try to get through the day without wanting to solve my life's problems all at once.

Just for today I will ... not try to correct or improve others, just myself.

Just for today I will be happy knowing that I am created for happiness.

Just for today I will change myself to fit the circumstances, not demand that circumstances change to fit me.

Just for today I will devote ten minutes to spiritual reading: as the body needs food so too my soul needs spiritual reading.

Just for today I will do a good deed and tell no one.

Just for today I will do something for which I have no taste; I will be content with that and will try to see that no one notices.

Just for today I will draw up an exact schedule....

Just for today I will believe — even when circumstances seem to contradict it — that God is there for me, just as though no one else existed.

Just for today I will not allow myself to be disheartened by the thought that I must hold out for a lifetime. I have twelve hours today for doing good.

I especially like this passage from St. Francis de Sales:

> "I am like a bird
> singing in the thornbush."

So I will speak little about my own sufferings; I will be restrained and indulgent in judging others; I will pray especially for those who have disappointed me, and in all things show great kindness and unlimited patience.

Certainly
there is nothing wrong
with speaking one's mind
at the appropriate moment,
but always with respect —
and a bit of humor,
so that no one feels hurt.

Seek not to know
who is right
and who is wrong.
Instead, seek reconciliation.

Meekness
is our strength.
It resolves every difficulty
and overcomes
every obstacle.

In dealing with others:
always maintain
dignity, simplicity,
graciousness — a calm,
cheerful graciousness.

Deploring evil is a disheartening task, and mere opposition to it will not make it go away. We must set our will against it and apply some energy to doing something about it.

We must proclaim goodness to the world, so that it can spread everywhere and in every possible way permeate individual lives and the entire community.

I thank the Lord for granting me a particular penchant for speaking the truth to everyone in every situation; with discretion and love of course, but with complete calmness and without fear. A few small lies from my childhood have left in my heart an abhorrence for double-dealing and lying. Especially now that I am older, I want most of all to be an honorable person....

Truth and love
must walk hand in hand.

See everything,
overlook much,
correct a little.

Listen to the full story
before passing
final judgment.

I will take as a fundamental principle to listen to everyone and everything with attention and reflection, form judgment slowly, without idle chatter or great outcry, with eyes wide open while not deviating from the precepts of the Church.

Peace requires
much understanding
and good will.
For even when
we like another person
there is always something
that one or another
finds displeasing.
That is when
godly patience,
the font of all blessedness,
is necessary!

Address of March 3, 1963

We all have our failings,
if not in one area
then in another.
We should be
accommodating to all.
To all — for in God's sight
they may be more
deserving than we.

If God is our Father,
then it follows that we all are
brothers and sisters
to one another.

God made us
not as enemies
but as brothers and sisters.

Encyclical from 29 June 1959

Human beings, not God, want war. They daydream about , defying every sacred law, thus making things even worse. The one who stirs this up is the "Prince of the World," who has nothing in common with Christ, the "Prince of Peace."

Diary, 1940

The world is poisoned by the unhealthy nationalism of blood and race, which stands in opposition to the gospel.... Our savior died for all nations, without distinction of race and blood; he has become the elder brother in the new human family founded on him and his gospel.

God is everything.
I am nothing.
That is enough for today.

Beware of self-praise and the desire to be regarded more highly than or even equally as well as others.

True, I am always at work, but in the depths of my being tend toward laziness and levity.... In my desire to be humble, I will keep on telling myself that I am a sluggard.

It would certainly be good for me to eat less than I have become accustomed. So I will halve my portions and for the most part drink less wine and add some water to it. As I think about this, perhaps I am promising too much. Yet I hope the Lord will help me keep true to my purpose and allow me some modest success.

Unfortunately,
this chair is big enough
for only half a nuncio.

*On a visit to the French Academy,
comparing the narrow chair to his
ample dimension, 1946.*

Everything
becomes easy
when we let go of ourselves.

Love above all else,
whatever the price.
For its sake
I would gladly
be considered a simpleton.

What a horse
cannot do,
a donkey can accomplish.

This is what it comes down to: always stirring oneself out of the established routine and looking for new approaches, ever open to the rightful claims of the age to which we live, so that in every way Christ can be proclaimed and made known.

To err is human.
But then we must
set things straight
immediately
and do better.

Address, 16 November 1960

I will respond
to any failing
with an act
of greater humility;
then I will begin again
with a joyful
and cheerful attitude
as if Jesus had
caressed me,
encouraged me and
personally comforted me.

I must try to control my tongue. I must be more restrained, especially in passing judgment on trusted persons.... I am by nature a very talkative person. That too is a gift from God. But it must be used with care and moderation....

An impression
about my inadequateness
never leaves me:
it is a great grace
from the Lord.
It helps preserve
my simplicity
and keeps me
from looking ridiculous.

My failures
and my wretchedness ...
keep me from
any manner of
self-exaltation;
but they do not weaken
my trust, my trust in God,
who places his gentle hand
over me, holding me
and giving me strength.

Knowing that we are children of God: this certainty is the unfailing spring of our joy....
It makes us sad to realize that God is so good to us while we are so unworthy. Still, even such sadness turns sweet.

Simplicity
contains nothing
that contradicts intelligence
— and vice versa.
Simplicity is love,
intelligence is thought.
Love prays,
the intellect watches.
"Watch and pray" (Mk 14:38):
perfect harmony.

The older I get the more I realize the value and overwhelming beauty of simplicity in thought, word, and speech.... Simplify all that is complex. As much as possible, reduce it to its original clarity without getting distracted by details.

A day without prayer
is like a sky without the sun,
a garden without flowers.

Praying
is like breathing.

Our brief intercessions
should be beyond counting!

My spiritual life can never go on vacation!

Pure prayer
is listening to God,
conversing with God
and being silent before God.

Address, 29 January 1960

I will not be a teacher of state-craft, of strategy, of science. There are plenty of them. I must be an advocate for truth and compassion.

Apart from the will of God, nothing holds interest for me.

Every month,
every day
belongs to the Lord.
That is why they are all
equally beautiful.

God does not look
at how *many* things I do,
but at *how* I do them.
He wants only my heart,
nothing else.

I live only
to obey God's will.

God knows
that I exist.
That is enough.

Divine providence
does not forsake
those who trust.

This is certain:
to the one who trusts
only in him,
the Lord gives
the right attire
for every kind of weather.

I do not save up
for the future.
Divine providence
will take care of it.
We honor him
by being thrifty
and helping others.

Avarice, no. Never.
Mortification, yes.

So that you may think of me this Christmas, I am sending you the last bit of money left over from my trip back from Italy. I have, so to say, shot my last bullet. Too bad, it was the only one I had left. I have used up too much ammunition this year.... But don't worry! I am a child of providence. And providence will not let you or me lack what we need.

Letter to his Family, 1927

The church is for everyone, but it must especially be the church of the poor.

Every parish
is my family photo album.

Part of a shepherd's job
is counting each
and every sheep.

Worries about the future out of self-love hinder God's action in us ... — and they are of no help at all in material concerns. Others may press forward and go further: I continue without haste right where the Lord has placed me and get out of their way. I wish to preserve my peace of mind, for therein lies my freedom.

Anyone can be pope.
I am the best proof of that.

I feel like an empty sack which the Holy Spirit suddenly and forcefully fills.

After his election as pope, 1958

Some expect the pope to be an able diplomat and statesman, others a man of learning.... Honorable brothers and beloved sons ... The new pope is, in view of his whole life, very much like Joseph, the son of Jacob, who calls in his brothers, after they suffered so much misfortune, and with great love and compassion reveals himself: ... I am Joseph your brother!

I am not
an important pope
like my predecessor,
I am not
a good-looking pope
— just look at my ears —
but you will get along
well with me.

Since the Lord has chosen me for this office (the papacy) without regard for my inner poverty, I sense that my life is no longer limited to a single issue.... The whole world is my family. This feeling of belonging to everyone must impress and enliven my spirit, my heart and my endeavors.

We want to get on well with one another. Let us gather with this attitude: let us try to discover what unites us and set aside whatever can divide us! When you return home, give your children a kiss and tell them it came from the pope!

Spontaneous greeting to
the crowd in St. Peter's Square,
11 October 1962

On the day after the papal election the archbishop charged with Vatican security came to John XXIII with the question of whether and when he would like to stroll in the Vatican gardens as his predecessors did.

Out of curiosity Pope John asked why he wanted to know this.

Because then the cupola of St. Peter's would have to be closed to visitors, came the answer.

Pope John replied: "Excellency, we promise you: during the stroll we will give no cause for scandal!"

Shortly after his election, Pope John visited the motherhouse of a religious congregation near the Vatican, where a former classmate lay seriously ill. The superior, completely flustered, wanted to introduce herself: "Holiness, I am the superior general of the Sisters of the Holy Spirit"; but in her confusion she got her words tangled and stammered: "Holy Father, I am the superior general of the Holy Spirit."

With quick wit John XXIII replied: "Oh, how wonderful! I am merely the vicar of Christ."

In answer to the question,
how many people worked
in the Vatican,
Pope John replied:
"About half!"

My guardian angel
often tells me:
John, don't take yourself
so seriously!

Approach everything with care, intelligence and with the simplicity of the gospel. People often expect even the pope's most commonplace assertions to be deep and mysterious. Yet much closer to the example of Jesus is an endearing simplicity that goes hand in hand with the cleverness of the wise and holy....

Once when Pope John was asked about the goal of the Second Vatican Council which he had called, he opened a window and said:

"Let some fresh air
into the church!"

To the objection of a prelate that it would be impossible to organize a council by 1963, Pope John responded:

> "Good, then let's open
> it in 1962!"

Without some
holy madness
the church cannot grow.

Tradition means:
protect the fire,
not preserve the ashes.

When I see
a wall between Christians,
I try to break off a brick.

The way to unity
between different Christian
confessions is love,
which unfortunately
shows itself too little
on either side.

Friendly feelings
toward our separated
Christian brothers and sisters
are not enough.
If we truly love them
we have to translate love
into action.

We do not want to start a jurid-ical process. We do not want to determine who is right and who is wrong. Both sides share the responsibility. We only want to say:

Let us come together
and put an end
to these divisions!

Address, 25 January 1959

That they may be one!

This is the intent of the divine redeemer, and we must carry it out.... That is the great task that lies before the conscience of every individual. On our last day at the particular and at the general judgment we will not be asked if we have achieved unity, but whether we have prayed, worked and suffered for it.

Christmas address, 1962

Our life on earth
is a journey.

With the passing years
come more farewells.
But a farewell
is only temporary.
We are all created
for heaven, and there
we will be reunited
in eternal joy.
The beautiful mansions
of this poor planet
pale in comparison!

We move toward heaven
from every different point
of the earth.
Yet
the path to get there
always follows the way
of the cross.

Knowledge of human frailty must inspire us to sympathy, comfort and encouragement for our neighbor. But we must not use it to excuse ourselves!

The small thorns
we endure out of love
for Jesus become roses.

In all honesty
let me say:
I hope to live a long life.
I love life!

Being calm
and ready for death
is the best way
to have a long life.

I have become so accustomed to think about death that it no longer holds any fear for me. For I know that heaven is much more beautiful than Venice and that the eternal festival of life will finally begin there ... as we meet our loved ones, who preceded us and now await us.

1955, as Patriarch of Venice

I must get used
to the thought of death,
so that my life
can thereby become
more happy, vigorous
and energetic.

A few decades ago a Franciscan author wrote that on this earth there is only one reason for complaint: the fact that we are not saints. If this inner drive and motivation is missing from our life, it is a serious deficiency. But if we have it, we gain for ourselves and for others joy and happiness while God's smile beams down on us.

Address, 21 January 1961

One can become holy
whether holding
a shepherd's staff
or a broom.

In my evening prayer I have this picture always before me: the crucified Jesus, spreading out his arms to embrace all. That is the task of the church, to fulfill the prayer of the Lord that all may be one.

31 May 1963, a few days before his death

If there is anything
that we need not repent
it is this:
in one way or another having
been too generous.

Sunshine On Our Way
99 Sayings on Friendship
ISBN 1-56548-195-X, 112 pp., hardcover

In preparation:
99 Sayings on Christmas

Organizations and Corporations

This title is available at special quantity discounts for bulk purchases for sales promotions, premiums, or fundraising.
For information call or write:

New City Press, Marketing Dept.
202 Cardinal Rd.
Hyde Park, NY 12538.
Tel: 1-800-462-5980;
1-845-229-0335
Fax: 1-845-229-0351
info@newcitypress.com